# PROFITABLE EVERGREEN

# NICHES

## For your blog & e-books

Kegesa Danvas Abdullah

# About The Author

Kegesa Danvas Abdullah is the founder of Cute Writers a professional copywriting Company and the Cute Online Money Empire.

I am an engineer, copywriter, web designer and content writer who is always ready for hire.

In case of any comments, questions, concerns, or corrections please contact:

danvkegesa@gmail.com

- My Blog
- Facebook
- Google Plus
- Twitter

**CLICK TO GET FREE EVERGREEN NICHE TOPICS**

# About this Book

This book aims to stop you from writing blindly.

Why?

Because:

- Not every e-book gets sold
- Not every blog gets visitors
- Not every author writes best-selling books

With this book, you shall focus your energy on topics that bring money.

This book is ideal for you if you are a writer who is looking for the most profitable niches. *It contains evergreen profitable niches which will always remain popular.*

After reading it, you will write e-books, books and content which people want to buy.

## To the eBook Writer (on Amazon or other e-book stores)

It will help you decide on the most profitable e-book niches

## To the Blogger:

It will help you choose the best and most profitable blogging niches

## To Authors:

It will help you know the hottest book topics which people want to buy

## Introduction

How will you feel if millions of people visit your website every month and convert into customers?

How will you feel if thousands of people buy and download your book daily?

You will feel good. Right?

Did you know that you have the power to attract customers just as you have power to write the best content ever?

Here is the good news:

"You can write evergreen content which people love reading always"

In this book, I am going to reveal to you the best evergreen writing niches that will stay evergreen forever and how to write or create articles, books and all manner of content for evergreen niches.

Sit back, grab some favourite beverage and let me explain this to you.

## What is Evergreen content?

Evergreen content is the type of content which remains relevant to people's day to day life situations. Evergreen content is the kind of content which people search regularly to solve their problems regardless the economic, political, climatic or any other factors.

People search for evergreen content always – they will not stop liking such type of content any time soon!

For example, content on health and fitness is always relevant to people every day. However, content on topics such as World War II is not always relevant to many people.

# What is The Real Meaning of

# Evergreen Content?

The word evergreen is used to describe vegetation which remains green regardless of seasons.

Evergreen trees or evergreen vegetation is always alive and green since they retain their leaves throughout all seasons regardless of the time of the year. Evergreen trees do not shed their leaves.

By inference, evergreen content is the kind of content which remains on demand always.

Evergreen content is the kind of content that generates traffic throughout its existence even without much promotion. However, the content must be properly written, actionable and well-optimized.

*"PROPERLY OPTIMIZED EVERGREEN CONTENT WILL ALWAYS GENERATE TRAFFIC THROUGHOUT THE YEAR"*

That said, it is important to know what does not constitute evergreen content. All content in the following categories is not evergreen:

- News
- Statistical reports
- Seasonal articles
- Festival reports
- Weather reports

- Election reports
- Sales articles
- Fashion articles

Evergreen content does not have an expiry date. People keep searching for evergreen content every now and again. Can you suggest any evergreen content topic?

Don't think too much, evergreen content entails facts and things which remain constant.

It is just like your favourite meal. You always feel like eating your best food any time of the day, month or year.

For example:

- The procedure for booting a specific type of an electronic device will remain constant always.
- Dating tips will always remain popular
- The principles of making money and becoming rich will always be demanded

# How to Write Evergreen Content

# Successfully

1. **Always look for pain points:** What are pain points? These are things which people are struggling to solve. Pain points are perennial in nature.

Examples of pain points:

**Losing weight**: Writing books or any type of content on "how to lose weight" will give you perennial traffic.

Beauty and appearance: All people, including you, want to look better. They will always demand solutions to their appearance. If you write on the following topics, you will get visitors forever:

- How to stay younger

- Acne remedies
- Removing pimples and staying smooth for good
- Removing wrinkles

Read on to find out more.

2. **Always target beginners:** Evergreen content is always best suited for beginners, not experts. Many experts do not look for help online.

For instance, you have seen content on topics such as:

- The Ultimate Beginners Guide to Blogging
- How to make Money Online as a Newbie Writer
- Affiliate Marketing for Beginners

3. **Use simple language:** Readable content is always ranked best. Make sure that your audience understands what you are putting across. What is the purpose of writing content which only you can read?

For instance, which of the following titles is easier to understand?

- Flabbergasting protocols of annihilating pimples
- Amazing ways of removing pimples

I see you now get the point. You need to be simple such that a grade 5 student can understand your writing without necessarily using a dictionary.

4. **Be specific in choosing your topic:** Being specific helps in creating evergreen content. Beginners love short and simple content since they don't have long concentration spans. Do not bore your readers before you give them value.

Always aim to address a specific problem. Avoid general knowledge.

5. **Build your content around a specific topic:** If you want your evergreen content to be great, choose a niche and build your content around it. Don't try to be a jack of all trades in one blog.

For example, instead of writing on how to make money, focus on how to make money online through article writing. This will help you get a targeted audience while beating your competitors.

6. **Create "How To" headlines of you are not sure:** Many how to topics are evergreen. For example, how to drive a bicycle will always remain factual. All you have to change is the brand of the bicycle and continue writing.

How to guides are great because they address recurring issues.

For instance, the process of starting a particular machine will always remain the same. Therefore, this is evergreen.

# Discussion on the Most Profitable Writing Niches

Now let's talk about the most profitable niches that will bring any blogger millions of profits through infinite number of visitors.

## 1. Money Niche

Who doesn't need money?

I have never come across anybody who hates money.

Money is a guaranteed search term in the internet.

You and I know why.

Money is scarce and important. It defines the kind of life you lead. The more money you have, the better.

You need money and that is why you are reading about the most profitable and evergreen niches.

You want to make a hell lot of it.

Now imagine telling people how to make money, shortcuts of making money, how to make money online, how to start an online business, how to save money and all sorts of ideas about money.

Won't you get many visitors to such a blog?

Yes.

That is why money is money niche is an evergreen writing topic which will always get you many searches and many visitors each month throughout the year.

To succeed in blogging about money, you got to teach people everything they want to hear about money.

Stay ahead of the game and tell them all money hacks that you know and you will always get traffic.

You will be telling people how to save and how to have more money if you want more visitors.

## 2. Sexual Matters

Many people love sex.

Its sweetness is inexplicable.

I love it. My friends love it.

What about you?

Sex builds marriages or destroys them (You know marriage is the fundamental institution which brings about families).

Telling people everything they need to know and do about their sex will be great.

The sex niche can be sub-divided into sex topics for ladies and sex topics for men.

Men like reading about:

- Strong erections
- Foods that boost sex

- Sex styles
- Boosting their masculinity
- Penis enlargement
- Building their sex drive and master their sex lives
- Premature ejaculation
- Stopping masturbation
- How to satisfy my wife

Ladies want to know:

- How to please their husbands in bed
- Taking care of their vaginas
- Sex positions to get pregnant
- Making their husbands enjoy sex

If you can assist both men and women overcome problems related with their sex life and make them have better quality sex, you will have lots of traffic to your blog.

# 3. The Food Niche

Who doesn't love food?

We all know that people and animals must eat to live.

***"Tell people what and how to eat well and they'll respect you."***

Therefore, any properly written article, blog or ebook on food will always be evergreen.

People will always want to cook and eat. They will check a few things like types of food, recipes, ingredients, preparation etc.

Writing a book about food will always bring you visitors.

Even if you niche down to Chinese dishes, Japanese dishes, Korean dishes, Indian dishes, English dishes, African dishes, etc., you must get buyers.

You can easily create food books by writing on some of the following topics:

- Foods for children or infants
- Foods for nursing mothers
- Foods for pregnant mothers
- Foods that have medicinal value
- Foods that enhance sexual performance
- How to cook various types of foods
- Recipes for various types/classes of people
- Foods for sick people (name all sicknesses)

It is important to note that any blog on food is bound to attract lots of traffic it is properly optimized for search engines and with good quality content.

## 4. Career Guidance

When will people stop working?

Not anytime soon.

In the contemporary society, people go to school and specialize in various academic fields. They need lots of career guidance.

Writing a book or starting a blog on career guidance is a clever way of attracting all people who need assistance in selecting careers. The niche is best for teachers and career counsellors. Visitors to career blogs include teachers, students, parents and career consultants.

At the moment, the competition in career guidance niche is fairly low and proper search engine optimization can easily see even a new career guidance blogger ranking well.

What about books?

The best thing about writing books on career guidance is the low competition and new careers which come every year.

For instance, news careers such as cryptocurrency studies, robotics, fintech need book writers to demystify a few things.

Why don't you take this opportunity and become an expert writer on such topics?

It is easy to give career guidance and it will be satisfying to see people successful as a result of your advice.

Instead of giving advice to people in your village or in your university only, why can't you start a career guidance blog or a career guidance ebook?

## 5. Jobs Niche

Everybody wants a nice job.

Thousands of people buy books on job-hunting daily.

An equal number of people visit job boards and job websites trying to look for jobs.

Information on how to secure dream jobs is scarce.

The need for writers to bridge this gap is ever-widening.

Everybody wants to get hold of any ideas which can help them get a better job.

People from all walks of life want promotions.

So, any quality books which will guide people on how to secure jobs will definitely have lots of sales regardless of weather, time of the year and economic conditions.

Some of the topics you will cover in this niche include:

- Resume writing tactics that will land you a job
- Writing a killer CV
- How to prepare for interview
- Firing your current boss and becoming big boss
- How to land your first job without experience
- How to make a nice first impression at interview
- How to fire bad workers
- How to know it is time to go for the next job

- Latest jobs in various fields
- How to defeat others in a job interview
- How to hire the best employees and many more.

As you can see, the list is endless and always evergreen. You are assured to sell many books or get lots of traffic to your website.

Could you be leaving money on the table of the jobs niche?

## 6. Sports

People love sports.

How many people buy TVs yearly because of sports?

For instance, do you know how many football fans live in your neighbourhood?

Sports attract an insane number of fans who want to consume your content.

You can excel as a sports writer because sports niche is evergreen.

I am not talking about sports news. I am talking about evergreen content on the sports niche. We already said that news articles are not evergreen since they keep changing every minute.

In this case, I am telling you about actionable content on sports.

If you follow the words in this guide, you shall start a nice sports blog.

All you have to do is to decide on any of the sports that you love most.

It is not advisable to write on all sports since you may not appear as an authority or expert in all sporting activities.

Just pick one sub-niche within sporting and write excellent and highly optimized content.

Join forums and see what sports fans are discussing.

You may wish to consider the following article topics:

- The ultimate football training guide
- How to become a good (sports person in your chosen sub-niche)
- Top 100 sports people of all time in (your niche)
- Training for sports, etc.
- Go sporty or die poor
- Becoming the best athlete

## 7. How to do anything (How-to Guides)

Many people don't like reading hard copy manufacturer's manuals about anything.

Instead, they want to read it from rea-life users.

They go online and search "how to...." On Google or any search engine of their choice.

Writing "How To" manuals can be a profitable blogging niche.

For instance, EHow and Wikihow thrive on making "how to" manuals that almost every internet user has stumbled upon.

Writing books in this niche will be surprise you. Even if you write a good book on how to train a baby to speak, how to eat pie, how to plant trees, how to become better, how to grow fat, etc., people will buy.

What you know could be somebody's nightmare.

They want to buy your books.

People even search insane things like "how to commit suicide, how to poison your wife or husband, how to cheat your spouse, how to kill your child, etc."

I am not saying you write books on such horrendous topics such as committing suicide. Just research what your target audience loves and tell them how to do it perfectly.

Secondly, you can research your passion and write what you love.

If your writing sounds good, people will always buy your books.

That's all for now!

## 8. Dating Tips

Most of us want to date in our lifetime. I am sure you agree with me.

This implies that dating is an evergreen niche.

You can write an excellent book about dating.

If you like this niche, you can also register your domain and start a blog advising people on everything about dating.

There are many experts in the dating niche but it is never ending.

Dating receives traffic from many younger people and some older people.

Young people look for dating advice on how to get spouses and how to please their spouses.

Did you know that dating never ends even after marriage for ideal couples?

The older guys may be looking for information on how to make their marriage work.

You will be surprised how many people look for books on dating advice on the internet.

Start writing books or articles in the dating niche and you shall get lots of customers in this evergreen:

- How to fall in love
- Dating guide for introverts/extroverts/shy people
- Gaining confidence to talk to the opposite sex
- How to get a good boyfriend
- How to get the best girlfriend
- How to start talking to a beautiful lady
- How to get a boyfriend within one day
- Dating tips/ advice for men and women
- How to love your wife or husband
- How to date the perfect man/woman
- How to get your ex back
- Dating venues for perfect dates

And everything imaginable about dating.

It will sell.

The list goes on and on and many people want your input.

# 9. Your Own Hobby

What is your hobby?

Do you think you are the only person who likes your hobby?

Just start write a book or articles about your hobby and publish your content.

Then sit and watch how many people are interested.

You will be shocked.

Examples:

If you love fishing as a hobby, write high quality articles or books about fishing and you will attract a community of people who love fishing as a hobby.

If your hobby if playing cricket, do the same, get customers and your income will definitely grow.

The good thing about hobbies, you will never be bored writing what you love.

You will always update your content and publish even more as people will always love hearing from somebody with whom they share interests.

Writing a hobby book works best if you are best in your hobby.

For instance, it will be difficult to convince people about football when you don't even know what it is all about nor any football player.

The point is this; make sure you have adequate information about your hobby so that your content becomes authoritative and compelling.

Take your time creating high quality content centred on your hobby and you will attract the right visitors.

## 10.   Health and Fitness Niche

More than 99% of people living on earth are really cautious about their health.

Aren't you cautious too?

It will be a nice thing to write about health and fitness.

Health and fitness is so broad that your blog may not accommodate all information.

It will be wiser to choose a sub-category within the health and fitness niche and concentrate on it.

Since specialists charge lots of money giving health and fitness tips or treating sick people, books covering the Do It Yourself (DIY) health and fitness issues get many customers.

A typical internet user will type on their computer something similar to the following keywords:

- How to lose belly fat really fast
- How to become fat within one month
- Homemade six-pack without gym

- How to have a nice shape
- Foods that burn belly fat
- Home remedies for belly fat
- How to treat ulcers by yourself
- Losing weight without exercise

I am sure you have searched the internet for a do it yourself health solution in the last couple of days. Maybe, you searched for something like "the best way to lose belly fat, how to get rid of some health problem, etc."

Imagine the number of people who are ready to pay for such content.

The trend is not going to stop any time soon.

That is why health and fitness is classified as an evergreen niche which will always attract lots of traffic.

All you have to do is to choose a sub-niche in the health and fitness niche and focus on it.

For example, arthritis.org publishes all things about arthritis. They get thousands of visitors per day looking for information about arthritis.

You can identify a challenge or an opportunity within the health niche and start sharing information.

Caution: Always share truthful information since health is a serious matter. You don't want to be sued for giving fake medical advice or for telling people to jump over dangerous places to lose weight.

You may decide to focus on the following sub-categories in the health and fitness niche:

- Weight loss and diets
- Nutrition and food preparation
- Diseases and prevention
- Wellness training and exercise

If done properly, health and fitness content can generate lots of traffic and lots of money for you.

## 11. Blogging Guide Niche

Ever since the creation of the first website, blogging has continued to grow.

Books and articles on blogging are always on high demand.

Many upcoming bloggers would love to hear how to set up a blog and make money from blogging.

Do not fear the number of books out there.

Grab this opportunity and write on blogging.

Show beginners how to get things right by giving no nonsense guides.

I always read about blogging because there are lots of things to learn to maintain a nice blog.

Whether one is a food blogger, personality blogger, health blogger, IT blogger or a blogger in any other niche, they must first learn how to blog.

All bloggers and upcoming web designers always read "how to blogs" to get information on how things are done. You shall agree with me on this.

Content on how to blog properly is important and evergreen all year round.

The best part of it, you can give advice to beginners, intermediate and expert bloggers on the same blog.

You can also incorporate serious lessons about search engine optimization, keyword strategy, how to monetize your blog, affiliate marketing and other digital marketing strategies.

Many people have earned a lot of money online by writing books or maintaining blogs on blogging.

It is important to offer unique content other than what others are giving.

## 12. Technology Niche

We all know that technology is here to stay.

Current trends show newer discoveries of modern technology each day.

People are eager to know what you have to say about the technology before they implement it.

They also want guides on "how to" do many things.

Technology is one of the best evergreen niches.

Instead of providing news about new technologies give your readers "how to guides"

Provide in-depth tutorials about any technology of your choice.

For example, you can write on robots, smartphones, laptops, and household electronic devices, televisions, androids, windows, Linux, radios and many more.

Millennials are interested in knowing how these stuffs work and how to use them. If you can provide up to date information to them, you will make sales.

Just like the blogging niche, technology has a lot of competition but niching down will give you an edge.

Proper optimization will always bring the required results.

## 13. Personality Development

Personality development is an evergreen niche.

Teach people how to know their identity and improve their self-worth and become better people.

All people want to know how to become better.

I bet nobody wants to be worse.

In this niche, you can teach people the psychology of life and how to improve themselves in what they do.

If you gain their confidence and offer quality content, you will always get visitors.

Be sure to check the following sub-categories in the personality development niche:

- Career development
- How to get rid of self-complexes
- Leadership development
- Life coaching
- Motivation guides
- Personality development
- Relation Ship Developments
- Self-esteem development
- Spirituality and personal growth

# 14. Internet Marketing

Internet marketing is a great evergreen niche for gurus who have adequate knowledge on consumer psychology, copywriting, search engine optimization, writing for the website, email marketing, digital marketing, and social media marketing and direct sales.

I am not trying to say that you cannot make it as a newbie writer.

All people grow from somewhere.

You can distinguish your books and content by filling the gaping holes in existing content.

You need to know much about how search engines work, SEO and how to create sharable content to succeed in this.

Internet marketing is always evergreen. People, businesses and large companies want to market their products online and they want to hear more about it. It is among the most searched niche and if you do it right, you shall get lots of traffic.

You may need some training to succeed in putting up a blog in internet marketing but be aware that it is great niche.

## 15. Product Reviews

Product reviews are best written as blogs as opposed to books.

However, you can write detailed books which review products.

Nobody will question that.

Many people like reading reviews before purchasing anything online.

Writing buying guides and product reviews will set your work apart from existing content.

A blog of reviews is an excellent evergreen blog which will always get targeted visitors.

The main advantage of writing reviews is "You can include your affiliate links and get commissions when people click on your links before purchasing"

What are you waiting for?

If you know how to write good reviews, go ahead and start a blog which reviews your favourite commodities.

You will surely succeed.

You can write reviews about services or goods.

Writing good reviews also helps in boosting your image as a reliable person.

Companies many also start contacting you to review their commodities once they realise that your blog attracts many readers.

All that is money and higher profits for you.

Once you set up a review blog or any other blog, it is always advisable to update it occasionally so that the tone of your writing suits the audience.

You may also tweak your blog to sound fresh.

## 16. All Diseases

Anything about diseases is evergreen.

Although diseases were mentioned under health, they deserve their own category.

Well, diseases are bad. Nobody really wants people to be sick so that you sell them medicine and get wealthy.

However, some homemade remedies provided by bloggers work far much better than modern medicine.

For instance, some herbs work well than over the counter medicine.

Many successful health bloggers sell or promote conventional herbal medicine.

I am here to tell you that you can start a successful blog which helps people on various types of diseases.
Just pick one that you want to expound on and write excellent content. You will get high traffic to your blog and you can start promoting medical stuff to your readers (not just medicine only).

## 17.     Weight Loss

There are many evergreen niches, but weight loss is one of the biggest and most popular.
 Site visitors are always searching for new weight loss tips, and search volumes are immense.
If you are just starting out, there are plenty of sales funnels, email autoresponder series and products to use.

Content in this niche is very easy to create, and if you're not much of a writer, you can get content written for you for about $3 an article.

## 18. Muscle Building

If losing weight is Step 1, gaining muscle tone has to be Step 2. Muscle building accompanies weight loss, and it mainly targets the male demographic.

For many online marketers, muscle building is one of the simplest evergreen niches to crack.

CPA offers for related supplements are an awesome way to monetize affiliate sites.

## 19. Dog Training

Every day, hundreds of people adopt dogs and need help learning to train them. The pet industry is a multi-million-dollar niche, and there's plenty of room for affiliate sites to help new pet owners, and you'll make plenty of money while you're offering advice.

## 20. Alternative Sources of Energy

This evergreen niche is one of the fastest-growing evergreen niches.

With fuel prices creeping back up, it's simple to see why so many people are looking for info on wind, solar power and other energy sources.

People will always need energy, and there will always be a market for those who want to know how to create their own electricity and save money.

The green living trend has become popular over the last 10 years.

This has been as a result of more environmental awareness among households and an active intervention by governments and non-profits organizations on the importance of green living.

Possible markets in this niche include:

- People that need to install solar panels
- People looking for green (non-pollutant) cars
- People looking to reduce their energy bills at home

Clickbank has lots of green living products you can choose to promote.

## 21. Online Income

This is likely the most searched for online niche, and it's simple to buy traffic.

The online income niche constantly has new informational products, and while it's not the best site for an IM newbie, it's a great evergreen niche for a seasoned marketer who's ready to build a strong list and earn a sustainable income.

## 22. Learning New Languages

Learning languages is also another evergreen niche you can target.

Language courses have some of the highest conversion rates in the online marketing industry, and they pay more than other informational product types.

A person learning a language typically does so out of necessity, which makes for the higher conversion rate. Good courses are in it for the long haul, and by providing a good one; you'll always have a source of profit.

You can build sites on how to learn French, Spanish, Italian and so on. Here, you have various monetization methods including product sales, training videos, membership sites among others.

## 23.    Parenting

As long as people continue to have children, the parenting niche will continue to be popular. It's evergreen because society continues to grow and evolve, and children's needs are changing along with it. The parenting niche is rather broad, containing topics from education to creative play to discipline, and there are tons of information products out there for you to build sites around or turn into an email series.

## 24. Finance

Everyone is looking for ways to improve their finances, but most people need a push in the right direction. There is an abundance of "get rich quick" literature online, but it should be viewed with a healthy degree of skepticism. If you're interested in helping people improve their finances, you should consider these points:

- 12 of the 20 most popular Clickbank products are income-related
- Personal finance books are regularly on top of Amazon's Best Seller list
- Many finance keywords have great search volume; "make money" has over three million searches per month!

Besides this niche being evergreen, there's another compelling reason why it's popular. When a person buys something that won't improve their finances, they regard it as expenditure. However, when they buy something that may help them increase their income, they see it as an investment.

## 25. Self Help/Self Improvement

The self-help niche is evergreen and very competitive because people are always on a quest for self-improvement.

In today's rushed, hurried and stressed-out society, people are looking for advice to improve their mind-set.

Capitalize on this by promoting digital courses along with tangible goods like supplements and aromatherapy candles. Who knows—you may even get rid of some of your own stress!

## 26. Make money online

Perhaps one of the largest evergreen niches is how to make money online.

Every day, hundreds of people are searching on how to make money online. Truth be told, this niche is hard to break into.

Happenings in the last couple of years that saw over-hyped products selling for thousands of dollars without resulting to

## 27. Photography

The photography niche is one of the niches that have immense opportunities for online marketers.

When people think of the photography niche, they mainly think of doing reviews of cameras and other products that can interest photographers.

However, you can go even further and create training products for a particular niche if you are a professional.

For example, how about starting a course about taking portraits?

How about training on all aspects of photography lighting?

## 28. Tattoos

The tattoo niche is also huge and offer different monetization avenues.

You can sell tattoo related products, target people who need to remove tattoos, sell DIY tattoo kits and so on.

The tattoo niche is an example of a passion and lifestyle niche.

The people who get tattoos are passionate about the products and will usually get more than one tattoo over a couple of years.

While some people love tattoos, others hate them. Nowadays, people have learnt the negative effects of tattoos and they may be interested in this:

- How to remove tattoos at home
- Removing tattoos very fast
- Cheapest ways of removing tattoos
- How to clear tattoos from your body

## 29. Parenting

This is a very broad niche that must be broken down to be well defined.

Parents will always have trouble with their children or face various issues when raising them.

You have to identify the particular problem that the parent may have and solve it.

Some of the ideas that come to mind in this niche include:

- Baby products
- Managing ADHD
- Dealing with disobedient children

## Last Remarks on Profitable Evergreen Topics

This book has shown you that there are many profitable evergreen niches you can exploit as a writer through blogging or book publishing.

All you have to do is to take the step now.

Choose a niche and start writing your way to riches.

Knowledge is useless unless utilized.

Remember that writing evergreen content is the best practice for writers who want to succeed in making profits from writing

Best regards in your writing career.

# CONTACT THE AUTHOR

**I am always available to work with you or for you.**

If you need help writing your book, you can hire me or my team of writers. We handle all types of writing tasks ranging from ghostwriting, article writing, ebook writing, novels, copywriting, web pages, etc.

In case of any comments, questions, concerns, or corrections please contact me: Cute Online Money

danvkegesa@gmail.com

Kindly, Show your Love by

**Writing a Genuine Review of This**

**Book**

www.ingramcontent.com/pod-product-compliance
Lightning Source LLC
Chambersburg PA
CBHW030524220526
45463CB00007B/2706